The Epic Inner Journey: The Choice is Yours

Getting to the *Heart* of the Matter

VOLUME II

"Trying to understand life without a deep study of oneself is like trying to comprehend a book without reading it."

Vernon Howard

Raseedra

Getting to the *Heart* of the Matter

© 2018 Raseedra

www.theosisbooks.net

Cover Art Joelle Paur

ISBN 978-1723076558
Printed in the United States of America.

Table of Contents

Preface..5

Introduction..7

Chapter 1   Thinking and the Heart............................11

Chapter 2   MIND…The Human Mental Apparatus.......31

Chapter 3   The Faculty of Memory............................45

Chapter 4   Exploring the Darkness Within You.............57

Chapter 5   Dispelling the Darkness Within You............73

Chapter 6   The Process of Reawakening to Reality.........89

Epilogue 107

Author Biography...113

Getting to the *Heart* of the Matter

PREFACE

"Read not to contradict, nor believe and take for granted, nor to find talk and discourse, but to weigh and consider."

Francis Bacon

The Epic Inner Journey: The Choice is Yours is meant to be read from front to back. The benefit received from reading this book will be greatly reduced if it is read out of sequence. After your first initial reading allow a few days and reread the book again. The rereading helps to reinforce the ideas that are being presented. The ideas presented in *The Epic Inner Journey: The Choice is Yours* provide a new mental platform from which you can begin to view yourself, life, and the world from an entirely new perspective. If you choose to integrate the ideas and instruction contained in this book into your life, your life will miraculously begin to change. Things that you may have once considered beyond your reach, such as Peace, Joy, and Happiness will begin to visit you more often. You will discover that Peace, Joy, and Happiness already reside *within* you, but have been hidden behind a tightly woven veil of lies and self-deception. As you gradually uncover, expose, and renounce the lies that you have unwittingly been telling yourself about yourself and the world, you set yourself free from what has kept you bound. *The Epic Inner Journey: The Choice is Yours* is simply a reminder that you DO have a choice. At any time, you can choose to leave the smothering confines of your old inner world behind and make a course for the New. A glorious New World already exists and patiently awaits your return.

"Every man has within himself a continent of undiscovered character. Happy is he who proves to be the Columbus of his spirit."

Johann Goethe

INTRODUCTION

"Each heart is a world. You find within yourself that which you find without. The world that surrounds you is the magic glass of the world within you."

Johann Lavater

Most powerful complex machines come with a detailed instruction manual. Generally, instruction manuals consist of detailed diagrams and precise wording describing how the machine is designed to be operated. If there is unfamiliarity with the meaning of the words found in the instruction manual or the meaning imputed to the words found in the manual are misinterpreted by the user, it is very likely that the user would not be able to operate the machine as it was originally designed to function. The user would be totally in the "dark" when it came time to operate the machine effectively. Attempting to operate a powerful machine without a full understanding of how the machine was originally designed to function would precipitate a situation where the user's life would be in danger and anyone who might be in close proximity.

Human beings are also powerful complex machines, obviously quite capable of doing an immense amount of damage to themselves, each other and the planet. Human beings have been in the "dark" when it comes to understanding how they were originally designed by Life to function. Fundamentally, there are two main reasons for the abominable state in which all of humanity now finds itself.

The first reason for the abominable state in which humanity now finds itself is a deeply entrenched self-centered attitude of entitlement which arrogantly proclaims that human beings have the ability and the right to choose how they direct their lives in whatever way they want. The tragic result of that deeply entrenched self-centered attitude of entitlement has spawned the rapidly disintegrating civilization that now encompasses the entire planet. As long as human beings persist in maintaining that highly toxic attitude the future of humanity is very doubtful. For the individual who has no interest in changing their self-centered abhorrent ways the information and instruction provided in this book will be of little value. Their heart has been hardened to point where they will remain subject to the darkened state of consciousness that now surreptitiously governs their lives.

As with any powerful complex machine it is vitally important that the meanings of the words being used in the instruction manual be clearly understood by the user. Without a clear-cut comprehension of what the words actually indicate the user of the machine will be unable to operate the machine as originally intended by the machine's creator. In addition, where a user of the machine *does* understand the operating instruction, but arrogantly assumes that they are more intelligent than the machine's creator and is unwilling to fully comply with the operating instruction, a tragic outcome is unavoidable.

The second reason the for abominable state in which humanity now finds itself is its long-standing complete lack of understanding and confusion as to how human beings were originally designed by Life to function. The foremost cause for this lack of understanding is due to a misinterpretation as to the true meaning of the words found in inspired literary texts. Inspired texts when accurately interpreted provide life-saving information and pragmatic instruction for the steadfast aspirant. Inspired literary texts when accurately interpreted by the aspirant provide valuable clues which will assist the aspirant as they journey toward their true Home.

The last few paragraphs you just finished reading provide an analogy that will help you better understand yourself and some of the underlying dynamics that are at play in the heart of human beings at the present time. As you observe these underlying dynamics at play in yourself you will discover that you are not required to remain under their life-depleting influences. You have a choice in the matter, BUT you must first be willing to adhere to the operational guidelines issued by the Designer of the Living Universe. As always, the choice is yours.

With the information and instruction found in this book you now have the foundational material that will assist you in gaining a more complete and deeper understanding of yourself. You will finally be… "Getting to the *Heart* of the Matter"

CHAPTER 1

Thinking and the Heart

What is *it* that provides the basis for all human behavior? The English philosopher James Allen in his book, *As a Man Thinketh,* suggested it is THINKING; making the following insightful statement, "As a man thinketh in his heart, so shall he be." Meaningful words truly worth considering. Words and their ascribed meanings provide the basis for all thought. We each possess a personal internal dictionary that we use to define ourselves, others and the world at large. How we perceive, interpret and view ourselves, others, and the world at large is determined by how the words in our internal dictionary are presently defined. Have you ever said something to someone that was intended to be completely harmless and the other person reacted defensively to what you just said? Perhaps the roles were reversed and you were the one who reacted defensively. What just happened? The words that were said were interpreted by each person using *their* personal internal dictionary. Possibly the words that were said were *thought* to be dismissive, threatening, condescending or any number of possible interpretations.

Have you ever thought something about yourself, another, or the world at large, which you discovered was limiting and untrue? Are you willing to start the process of honestly examining the definitions given to the words in your personal internal dictionary and relinquish any definitions that are discovered to be limiting and untrue? Any unwillingness to fearlessly examine the verity of the contents of your personal internal dictionary will guarantee that you will needlessly continue to repeat the past over and over again.

> "Remember that it is not the man who gives blows or abuse who offends you, but the view you take of these things as being offensive. When, therefore anyone provokes you, be assured that it is your own opinion which provokes you."
>
> Epictetus

> "You can remove out of the way many useless things which disturb you, for they lie entirely in your opinion towards them."
>
> Marcus Aurelius

"This pulling out of imagination which I am recommending, will also forbid us to summon up memory of past misfortune, to paint a dark picture of the injustice or harm that has been done to us, the losses we have sustained, the insults, slights, and annoyances to which we have been exposed, for to do that is to arouse fresh life into all those hateful passions long laid asleep – the anger and resentment which disturb and pollute our nature."

Arthur Schopenhauer

James Allen doesn't define what he meant when using the word *heart*. So, what is the heart? Clearly, James Allen considered the heart to be pivotal to the process of thinking and the repository for what ultimately determines the disposition of an individual; "…so shall he be." A repository is a place where things are deposited and stored; a storehouse. The word commonly used to identify the human mental apparatus is the word *MIND*; the faculty wherein the process of thinking takes place within the individual. What is not generally recognized is that the human mental apparatus is an ultra-sophisticated TWO-PHASE mechanism.

The design of the human mental apparatus consists of two fundamental parts or phases, which will be designated in our consideration as simply the MIND PHASE and the MEMORY PHASE. The mind phase is where the process of thinking takes place and is experienced, while the memory phase stores the information which provides the basis for our thoughts and feelings. The memory is the faculty which has the ability to store as thoughts and feelings the complete personal history of an individual. What is truly remarkable is that the faculty of memory has the ability to record the full range of sensory input associated with a particular event, what you experienced through your five senses, all of the sensory feelings you experienced that were associated with that particular event get recorded in memory. Regard the memory as an archive that contains a vast collection of "files," a full-blown, multimedia record of your entire personal history, starting at birth and continuing seamlessly up to the present moment. Keep in mind as we proceed the following important fact in relationship to yourself: *What is stored in your faculty of memory is nothing but the PAST!*

> "The fictitious me is an accumulation from the past. All that has been accumulated becomes the "me"

sense. Only by dispelling this accumulation does the sacred present itself."

Adyashanti

It would be absolutely impossible to think if your memory was suddenly erased. Likewise, a computer without a memory would be a useless assemblage of parts. The human mental apparatus is an extremely complex mechanism, a "bio-computer," designed by Life for a specific purpose. Obviously, it is not necessary to understand how every part of the bio-computer works before we can think. When using a computer, car, television, lawn mower, cell phone, or any other mechanical contrivance, in each case it was not necessary for you to completely understand how each of these complex mechanisms worked before you could use them. All that was required was an interest in gaining a basic understanding as to what was required to operate the mechanism properly, and then follow the instructions. An instruction manual usually accompanies most complex mechanisms which clearly outlines how to properly operate the mechanism. As we are all well aware, in the case of the human mental apparatus, an instruction manual was not included when being born into the world. When it comes to understanding how to properly operate the human mental apparatus, human beings have clearly remained in the dark for an extended period of time. The tragic conditions that presently exist in the world bear witness to that fact. Without a basic understanding as to how the human mental apparatus was *originally* designed by Life to be operated, and a willingness to follow those instructions, human beings will needlessly continue to go through life wondering what Life is about, and why as human beings we continue to behave in such irrational and self-destructive ways.

In order to restore a highly sophisticated apparatus which the Mind *is*, the first requirement is to have a basic understanding as to how that apparatus was originally designed to function and be operated. Once that basic understanding is acquired and acknowledged, then each person has a choice to make. They can either willingly follow the operational guidelines established by Life for the operation of the Mind, or they can willfully choose to ignore them.

In the biblical story of the Garden of Eden, Man, signifying both man and woman, are forewarned of the tragic consequences that would befall them if they chose to violate the operational guidelines as they pertain to the operation of their mind. The warning can be found by reading Genesis 2:17. Man was instructed to abstain from using the limited knowledge he possessed for determining and making judgments as to what was "good" and what was "evil." *Judging what is good or evil requires the operation of one's MIND!* According to the story, Adam and Eve chose to ignore the warning and continued to judge. Tragically, human beings continue to ignore that original instruction and continue judging. The tragic saga that is now unfolding on Earth is simply the cumulative effect of countless generations of human beings failing to follow the operational guidelines for the operation of their mind. The allegorical story of the *Fall of Man* found in the first chapter of the Bible describes the tragic consequences that result when human beings choose to violate and ignore the established operational guidelines for the human mental apparatus.

Thinking would be impossible without the faculty of memory and the faculty of memory would be purposeless without the faculty of mind. The composition of the thoughts and feelings we experience in any given circumstance will be determined by the thoughts and feelings we *already* have recorded in memory. The thoughts and feelings we have towards a given circumstance will govern our behavior. Behavior patterns have both an internal and overt component. Internal feelings such as anger, resentment, frustration, fear, worry, rage, etc; along with the thoughts associated with those feelings are examples of internal behavior patterns, they are experienced internally, while punching a hole in a wall with your fist is an example of an overt behavior pattern. At present most individuals behavior patterns both internal and overt are strictly governed by the thoughts and feelings that were *previously* recorded in their memory and have become largely automatic and involuntary; performed robotically without conscious thought. A very large percentage of our automatic, robot-like, behavior patterns are the direct result of traumas we have experienced throughout our life. It could easily be asserted that by the simple fact of our being born into this crazed man-made world we are bound to experience one trauma after another, starting at our birth and ending when we have taken our last breath. The word *trauma* refers to any physical/mental/emotional wound or shock that creates substantial lasting damage to one's psyche. When the thoughts and feelings surrounding a particular traumatic event get firmly implanted in memory they provide the starting point for future involuntary behavior patterns when they are triggered. When a person's behavior patterns become involuntary, automatic, habitual, robot-like, they have at that point abdicated their innate ability to consciously choose their behavior. They needlessly live in an unconscious, self-induced, limited and diminished, somnolent state, that is completely governed by their past…what is stored in memory. Your personal experience of life is determined by how you think and feel. How you think and feel is determined by the mass of information you have acquired and assimilated throughout your life and is now stored in memory as your personal history. Your personal history and who you think and feel *you* are, (the "me" sense) are one and the same. To begin the process of understanding yourself and others, it is crucial that you first understand how the faculty of memory functions.

The word *heart* referenced by James Allen is analogous to the faculty of memory working in concert with the faculty of mind. The *contents* of the faculty of memory (heart) will ultimately determine and condition what is brought forth and experienced in a person's life, "…so shall he be." The content of the faculty of memory acts as a "filter" through which a person perceives and interprets the world, also, providing the basis for who you think and feel you are. In the King James Version of the Bible according to Answers.com the word *heart* appears 830 times! For the heart to be mentioned that often suggests that a greater understanding of how the heart (faculty of memory) functions is paramount to gaining a greater understanding of oneself. The following Bible verses succinctly summarize the vitally important role of the heart. "A good man out of the good treasure of his heart bringeth forth that which is good; and an evil man out of the evil treasure of his heart bringeth forth that which is evil." Luke 6:45. "For out of the abundance of the heart the mouth speaketh." Mathew 12:34. What is stored in a person's heart is its content. When substituting the word *content* for the word *abundance* the above bible verse takes on a revelatory new meaning: 'For out of the *content* of the heart the mouth speaketh.' *It is the actual content of a person's heart (faculty of memory) that determines what is experienced and brought forth in a person's life.* Please, stop reading for a moment. Now, slowly reread the *italicized* sentence, substituting the word *"my"* for the words *"a person's."* It is vitally important that you recognize the absolutely definitive role *your* faculty of memory (heart) plays in determining how you presently interact with every aspect of your environment and how the content of your memory provides the sole basis for your current sense of identity. How an individual interprets and responds to their environment is governed by what is contained in their faculty of memory.

> "Each one sees what he carries in his heart."
> Johann Goethe

What singularly distinguishes human beings from the other creatures that populate planet earth? Fundamentally, it boils down to their ability to choose, to make conscious choices. The present state of the world clearly reflects the prior misguided choices made by untold generations of human beings and the resulting effects of those choices. There is no reason to judge the effects, they are what they are. Rather than judging the effects, a wiser course of action would be to investigate the *cause* of these effects and discover why the effects keep repeating themselves. Effects always follow causes. There *is* a reason why human history repeats itself, and it's in plain view for anyone who is willing to honestly examine the content of their faculty of memory, their heart. It is the content of a person's faculty of memory that strictly regulates and governs how a person interprets and responds to each moment to moment circumstance. The content of a person's faculty of memory will determine how that particular individual thinks towards a particular circumstance. How a person thinks about a circumstance will determine their behavior in relationship to that circumstance. Their behavior will determine the outcome, what is subsequently experienced and brought forth.

> "Whatever we are now is the result of our acts and thoughts in the past; and whatever we shall be in the future, will be the result of what we think and do now."
> Vivekananda

> "Happy is he who has been able to learn the cause of things."
>
> Virgil

The process of thinking requires both the faculty of mind and the faculty of memory (heart) working in concert. In today's world a person's intellectual prowess is defined by the amount and quality of the information they have accumulated throughout their life. The information they have accumulated throughout their life is stored in their faculty of memory which singularly provides the bytes of information necessary to engender their thinking process. This voluminous storehouse of information constitutes the total infrastructure of a person's intellect and at the same time provides the basis for their sense of identity, who they think and feel they are. The Age we currently live in is commonly referred to as the Information Age, where intellectual knowledge is regarded as all-knowing and all-powerful. The dire state observed in the world today is the direct result (effect) of man's misuse and misapplication of his capacity of intellect; unfailingly reproducing and perpetuating the same tragic human drama over and over again. Countless generations of human beings have blindly ascribed to the deeply ingrained belief that the human intellect is capable of solving the problems its very misuse and misapplication has created. Albert Einstein, one of the most creative geniuses of our time had this to say about solving the problems mankind now faces: "We cannot solve our problems with the same thinking we used when we created them." Additionally, he said, "Insanity is doing the same thing over and over again and expecting different results." To paraphrase Einstein's words, *'It is human being's repetitive and insane THINKING that perpetuates and sustains the problematical and troubled state being experienced by mankind.'* Could it be that man's misuse of the revered and exalted human intellect is at the core of every problem that now confronts mankind? Let us take it a step closer to home. Are *you* willing to entertain the possibility that the content of *your* intellect is at the core of every problem that confronts you personally? Each person must answer that question for themselves. How *you* choose to answer that question will ultimately determine the fate of *your* world. Similarly, the fate of humanity will be determined by how mankind collectively chooses to answer that question. Failure to start the process of questioning the verity of the content of one's intellect will guarantee that the past keeps repeating itself over and over again. Remember, it is the content of one's intellect that governs their behavior. Our patterns of behavior determine what is experienced and brought forth in our life. Human consciousness, both individually and collectively (mass consciousness), is shaped by the thoughts and feelings that constitute the makeup of the human intellect. The present troubled state of the world is simply the out-manifestation of the troubled state of human consciousness. In order for the troubled world situation to change it will first require the restoration of human consciousness. The restoration of human consciousness precedes the restoration of the planet.

How is the restoration of human consciousness to be accomplished? The first step in the restoration process of any item is to acknowledge the *actual condition* of the item being restored. In the case of the human consciousness the first step is exactly the same. You must be willing to honestly acknowledge the actual condition of *your* intellect, which singularly provides the basis for your present state of consciousness. The condition of your intellect is determined by the mass of information that is currently stored in your faculty of memory, which provides a complete detailed record of your personal history. Your personal history is a multifaceted collage composed of all your acquired beliefs and their associative feelings. The Greek sage Epictetus makes reference to the condition of a person's mind (intellect) in the following quote. "The beginning of philosophy is to know the condition of one's own mind. If a man recognizes its weaknesses, he will not wish to apply it to important questions." The word *philosophy* refers to the rational investigation of the truths and principles of Being. What currently makes up the condition of *your* mind? How you presently interpret and view yourself, others, and the world at large is solely based upon the condition of your mind. It is this heterogeneous and incongruous mass of acquired information, comprised of your personal thoughts and feelings, that provides the basis for the lighting-fast operation of the intellect. This mass of acquired information that comprises the intellect remains largely static until "triggered" by the circumstances we encounter as we journey through life. Similarly, the mass of information stored in the memory of a computer remains static until it is retrieved for a specific computation. How an individual responds to a given circumstance will be strictly governed by the lightning-fast operation of their intellect in relationship to that particular circumstance. A person can respond to a circumstance in one of two ways, either consciously or unconsciously. When a person's response to circumstance becomes involuntary, automatic, habitual, a "knee-jerk" reaction, at that point the person is no longer acting consciously, colloquially speaking they are "asleep at the wheel."

"The greatest part of mankind…may be said to be asleep, and that particular way of life which takes up each man's mind, thoughts and actions, may be very well called his particular dream. The degree of vanity is equally visible in every form and order of life. The learned and the ignorant, the rich and the poor, are all in the same state of slumber."

William Law

"While they dream, they do not know that they are dreaming."

Lao-tse

" Nothing is more hidden from us than the illusion which lives with us day by day, and our greatest illusion is to believe that we are what we *think* ourselves to be."

Henri Amiel

"As a man in his sleep doubts the reality of his nightmare and yearns to awaken and return to real life, so the average man of our day cannot, in the depths of his heart, believe the terrible condition in which he finds himself - and which is growing worse and worse – to be a reality. He yearns to attain a higher reality, the consciousness of which is already within him…Our average man has but to make a conscious effort and ask himself, 'Is not all this an illusion?' in order to feel like an awakened sleeper, transported from the hypocritical nightmare-world into a living, peaceful, and joyous world of reality."

Leo Tolstoy

If you want to wake up, the first thing you need to seriously consider is that you are asleep and everything you take as real is a dream."

Adyashanti

What are William Law, Lao-tse, Henri Amiel, Leo Tolstoy, Adyashanti, and a host of other noted thinkers intimating when they proclaim that human beings are asleep? Certainly, they are not referring to the act of lying in bed with one's eyes closed. For these men and others to say that human beings are asleep, dreaming, slumbering, and living in a horrible nightmare-world; how is that possible? With only a basic understanding of how the human mental apparatus functions it is possible to understand what these noted thinkers are attempting to communicate to slumbering humanity.

Getting to the *Heart* of the Matter

CHAPTER 2

MIND...The Human Mental Apparatus

> "At bottom there is but one subject of study...the mind. All other subjects may be reduced to that; all other studies bring us back to this study."
>
> Henri Amiel

Let us apply the KISS Principle (Keep It Simple Stupid) to our understanding of the human mental apparatus. The human mental apparatus is a highly sophisticated device designed and produced by Life to perform a specific function relative to the ongoing creative processes here on earth. Without the human mental apparatus, it would be impossible for human beings to interface with their environment. Clearly, the operation of the human mental apparatus plays a pivotal role in determining what ultimately transpires and is brought forth on planet earth. Take a moment and look at all the *man-made* objects in your immediate environment. It is not difficult to acknowledge that each man-made object was the direct result of someone thinking about it first. Obviously, the human mental apparatus plays a pivotal role in the bringing forth of man-made objects. Now, take a moment and look at all the objects in your immediate environment that are part of the *natural world*. How willing are you to entertain the mind-boggling possibility that the bringing forth of the objects in the natural world was also the direct result of the operation of the human mental apparatus? Is it possible that human beings were *originally* designed by Life with that sole purpose in mind; to facilitate and take part in the ongoing creative activities relative to planet earth? If human beings were originally designed by Life with that purpose in mind what happened? Plainly, the natural world when left unmolested by man gives evidence of an orderly, living design, that seamlessly blends with the cosmos; a unified, harmonious whole, comprised of countless interrelated components. The present troubled state of the world is the direct result of the continued misapplication and misappropriation of the human mental apparatus by human beings. There is no other rational explanation for the present dire condition of the world. If you have ever asked the question, "WHY? Why is the world the way it is?" …the reason was just revealed to you.

> "For the outward world is but a glass, a representation of the inward; and everything, and variety of thing in temporal nature, must have its root or hidden cause in something more inward."
>
> William Law

What is this inward "something" which William Law is referring to within each individual that strictly governs what manifests outwardly in their lives? James Allen's insightful quote holds the key to understanding why the world is the way it is. "As a man thinketh in his heart, so shall he be." It is the *content* of the heart (faculty of memory) that governs a how each person thinks. It is their patterns of thought and feeling that in the final analysis determines *what shall be.* The man-made world human being have created on the surface of the planet is simply a reflection, an out-manifestation of the contents of the collective heart of mankind. For those of you who wish to see first hand what is actually contained in the collective heart of mankind all that is required is to watch the evening news and peruse the World Wide Web. Not a very pretty picture. Man's continued misapplication and misappropriation of the human mental apparatus is the root cause for EVERY problem that now confronts mankind, both individually and collectively.

A television set is a device designed by man to provide a mechanism for the conversion of the invisible TV signal into a visible picture. Similarly, the human mental apparatus was designed by Life to provide a mechanism for the unified and harmonious interface between the invisible (non-dimensional) and visible (dimensional) phases of Being. Ralph Waldo Emerson had this to say about the interface between the invisible and visible phases of Being. "Man stands in strict connection with a higher fact never yet manifested. There is a power over and behind us, and we are the channels of its communication." It is very important to keep in mind that the human mental apparatus is a highly sophisticated device designed by Life for this specific purpose.

> "Every instrument, tool, and vessel, if it does that for which it has been made, is well, and yet he who made it is not there. But in the things which are held together by nature there is within and there abides in them the power which made them; therefore, the more it is fit to reverence *this* power, and to think that if thou dost live and act according to *its* will, everything in thee is in conformity to *its* intelligence."
>
> Marcus Aurelius

All devices regardless of how simple or sophisticated are designed by their creator with a specific purpose in mind. Additionally, all devices are designed by their creator to be operated in a specific way. For example, a Honda Accord was designed to be operated on paved streets; it was not designed to be operated as a farm tractor. If a Honda Accord was employed as a tractor by a farmer, it would not be long before the Accord broke down due to the farmer's misapplication and misappropriation. The failure of the farmer to operate the car according to its original operational guidelines precipitated the car's eventual breakdown. Likewise, there are specific operational guidelines that relate to the proper operation of the human mental apparatus. When the original operational guidelines of the human mental apparatus are misapplied and misappropriated by human beings, calamity is the unavoidable result to both the operator and the operator's environment. The present troubled state of the world bears witness to that fact. In the case of human beings, the scope of the calamities includes a few of the following: physical, mental, and emotional breakdown of the individual, wars, ecological degradation, water, air, and soil pollution, extinction of entire species of plants and animals, etc.

The world-wide breakdown that mankind is now experiencing is the cumulative effect of countless generations of heedless human beings continued misapplication and misappropriation of the human mental apparatus. [NOTE: As we proceed in our investigation into the workings of the human mental apparatus the following words should be considered as synonymous; heedless, unconscious, deluded, asleep, slumbering, and dreaming. When you come across one of these words as you read, experiment by substituting one of the other words in its place. The practice of substituting one word for another will help augment your understanding of the ideas being presented.] In the above example of the farmer continuing to operate the car as a tractor, we have an example of how a heedless human being behaves. The question begs to be asked, 'Why would anyone continue to behave in such a careless and destructive manner?' The breakdown of the Honda Accord was completely unnecessary and avoidable if the farmer had merely followed the car's operational guidelines. Are you willing to tentatively acknowledge that the present troubled state of the world is the direct result of countless generations of heedless human being's failure to follow the operational guidelines for the human mental apparatus?

> "Who is more deluded than he who is careless of his own welfare?"
>
> Shankara

The troubled state of the world clearly reveals that human beings have been careless of their own welfare for an extended period of time. A brief study of human history reveals that human beings have been careless when it comes to their own welfare and that of the planet. The words, slumbering, dreaming, unconscious, asleep and deluded have been used by some of the world's greatest thinkers, prophets and sages to identify and expose the reason *why* human beings continue to carelessly behave as they do. The repeated vilification or elimination of many of the world's greatest thinkers is indicative of mankind's reluctance to address the depth and severity of their own self-deception. For an individual or a group of individuals to mindlessly continue to repeat the same careless behaviors over and over again, is, as Albert Einstein said, a mark of insanity.

> " Nothing is so easy as to deceive one's self, for what we wish to believe we readily believe, but such expectations are often inconsistent with the real state of things."
> Demosthenes

To acknowledge that the world is insane is quite easy; to begin to suspect that oneself is insane, well, not so easy. For the purposes of this book the word *insanity* will be defined as follows: *Any pattern of thought and feeling that precipitates a corresponding internal or overt behavior pattern which is found to be deleterious to oneself, others, and the environment; that is subsequently repeated by that same individual or group of individuals.* The key to gaining an understanding as to why human history systematically repeats itself is found by first identifying the mechanism *within* the individual where these repetitious patterns of thought and feeling originate and how this mechanism actually functions. Once the mechanism is identified, and how it functions understood, then the appropriate adjustments can be instituted by the individual to ensure that the troublesome conditions do not repeat. For example, a man goes to a tire shop complaining that the right front tire on his car keeps going bald prematurely; he has replaced the tire several times in the last few months. The owner of the tire shop immediately understands the *cause* of the problem. He explains to the owner of the car that the mechanism that keeps the tires aligned has fallen out of alignment and needs to be adjusted. At that point the owner of the car has a choice to make, he can continue to operate his car as it is, or he can *choose* to make the necessary adjustments. Correspondingly, with your new insight and basic understanding as to how the human mental apparatus functions, you realize that *you* as the sole operator of this mechanism are responsible for any adjustments that need to be made; the choice is yours. THE CHOICE IS YOURS! With your new basic understanding of the how the human mental apparatus functions, you now have the foundational information which will allow you to start the process of bringing your life back into alignment with Life's Design. No longer will you needlessly be subject to the delusory and insane patterns of thought and feeling that have thus far undetectably governed your life. It is nothing but our heretofore unconscious acceptance and reliance on these deeply ingrained, robot-like, habituated patterns of thought and feeling, that keep us insulated and separated from the experience of our true nature as participating members in Life's harmonious Grand Design.

> "Nothing has separated us from Life but our own will, or rather our own will *is* our separation from Life. All the disorder and corruption, and malady of our nature, lies in a certain fixedness of our own will, imagination, and desires, wherein we live to ourselves, are our own centre and circumference, act wholly from ourselves, according to our own will, imagination and desires. There is not the smallest degree of evil in us, but what arises from this selfishness, because we are thus all in all to ourselves."
>
> William Law

If, "our own will *is* our separation from Life," then what is it that constitutes the will in an individual? Logically, the will has to be "something" that exists within an individual, or there would "no thing" to maintain their separation from Life. So, what is the will? What a person expresses, what they think, say, and do, is commensurate with the exercise of their will. What a person expresses is governed by how that person thinks and feels. When substituting the word *thinking* for the word *will*, the above quote takes on a profound new meaning. 'Nothing has separated us from Life but our own *thinking,* or rather our own *thinking* is our separation from Life.' How a person thinks and the exercise of their will are one and the same…thought-in-action. Where does the will originate and reside within an individual? The human mental apparatus is where the process of thinking takes place and is experienced; correspondingly, it is also the seat of the will. Thinking would be impossible without the faculty of memory to provide the bytes of information that go into the formation of a thought. The mass of acquired information that resides within a person's faculty of memory will predispose and govern how that person thinks; also, at the same time, provide the basis for what that person wills; how they express themselves. How can our own will be the *cause* of our separation from Life? It is through the exercise of their will that human beings either include or separate themselves from Life's all-inclusive harmonious design. The exercise of our will and our patterns of behavior are one and the same. How an individual or a group of individuals choose to behave in relationship to the circumstances they encounter as they journey through life will govern the quality and nature of the relationship they have with Life. In our examination of will, it is vitally important that you recognize the prime and pivotal role the faculty of memory plays in determining the *causal* relationship you not only have with yourself, but also your relationship with others and the world at large. There is a direct one-to-one relationship between what is contained in a person's faculty of memory and the makeup of one's state of consciousness. It is the makeup of our state of consciousness that regulates and governs the operation of our personal will.

> "But this is the fact which we have hitherto lost sight of; and since our perception of life is the measure of our individual consciousness of it, we have imposed upon ourselves a *world of limitation*, a world filled with

the power of the negative, because we have viewed things from that standpoint."

Thomas Troward

By gaining a deeper understanding how the human mental apparatus functions *within* you, you take the crucial first step in the process of freeing yourself from the "world of limitation" that has heretofore undetectably and chronically colored your perception of yourself, others and the world at large. Without a basic understanding of how the human mental apparatus functions in relationship to yourself, there is no way to see behind the curtain of lies and self-deception that you have unknowingly allowed to surreptitiously govern your life. The curtain can be rent, but before that can happen, you must first have a basic working knowledge as to how the human mental apparatus functions. Let us now dig a little deeper into how the human mental apparatus functions; more specifically, the faculty of memory. By gaining just a basic understanding of how the faculty of memory operates *within* you, you will be fostering a greater understanding of yourself. The greater your understanding of how the human mental apparatus functions, the greater your opportunity to free yourself from the "world of limitation" that you currently live within.

> "The first reason for man's inner slavery is his ignorance, and above all, his ignorance of himself. Without self-knowledge, without understanding the workings and functions of his *machine*, man cannot be free, he cannot govern himself and he will always remain a slave and the plaything of the forces acting upon him"
>
> George Gurdjieff

> "Know thyself."
>
> Socrates

CHAPTER 3

The Faculty of Memory

An individual *can* free themselves, but first, they must be willing to honestly acknowledge the actual condition of their own inner nature; their current mental and emotional makeup. To repeat William Law, "The beginning of philosophy is to know the condition of one's mind. If a man recognizes its weaknesses, he will not wish to apply it to important questions." To honestly acknowledge the actual condition of your inner nature requires a resolute willingness on your part to impartially observe your "weaknesses." To impartially observe yourself simply means, you non-judgmentally watch your patterns of thought and feeling as they arise and pass through your mind. Your weaknesses are made-up of nothing more than the unrecognized distorted and discordant patterns of thought and feeling that you have here-to-fore unknowingly allowed to govern your life. Your inner nature, your "state of consciousness," is inseparable from the mass of information that is currently recorded in your faculty of memory; they are one and the same. A severely fragmented inner nature is simply the toxic by-product of a faculty of memory which is filled with distorted and discordant information. When this toxic mishmash of faulty information is permitted to govern an individual's life, tragic consequences are the inevitable end result. The word *tragic* best describes the present state of the world. The present tragic condition of the world is the end result of countless generations of human beings obliviously permitting this toxic stew of pernicious information to continue to govern their lives; thus, reproducing the same tragic state of affairs over and over again. In the last sentence the word *oblivious* was used. The following list of terms is a small sampling of the synonyms for the word oblivious, taken from Dictionary.com: asleep, deluded, unthinking, ignorant, absentminded, unconscious, heedless, unaware, unwitting, careless, unsuspecting, mechanical, blind, unseeing, incognizant, haphazard, comatose, in the dark, and dreaming. As was mentioned earlier, many of the world's greatest thinkers have used these very same terms to describe the human condition. Why? What vital information do you suppose they are attempting to convey to their circle of listeners? Who is willing to not only listen, but to honestly investigate and consider these terms in relationship to oneself and whether what is being suggested by these great thinkers and sages is in fact true?

> "Nothing has such power to broaden the mind as the ability to investigate systematically and truly all that comes under your observation in life."
>
> Marcus Aurelius

> "Every night we should call ourselves to account: 'What weakness have I overcome today? What passions opposed? What temptations resisted? What virtue acquired?' Our weaknesses will decrease of themselves if they are brought every day to the light."
>
> Seneca

> "Observe yourself as your greatest enemy would do; so, shall you be your greatest friend."
>
> Jeremy Taylor

With persistent practice it is possible to observe our thoughts and feelings as they arise and pass through our mind. When a person is said to be *awake* the thoughts and feelings that arise in each moment are in direct response to the immediate circumstance. Conversely, when a person is said to be *day dreaming* they are for the most part totally unaware of what is going on around them. They are lost in a private world of fanciful thoughts and feelings that do not correspond to the immediate circumstance. Whether a person is said to be awake or day dreaming the source of their thoughts and feelings in both cases arise out of their faculty of memory. As long as a person is alive there is not a moment when their faculty of memory is not operative. Moment by moment, it is the content of our memory that not only influences and governs how we interface with others and the world, but also oneself. How we *see* ourselves, commonly referred to as our *sense of identity,* is determined and governed by the content of memory. Clearly, if a person's faculty of memory was blank they would have no basis for a sense of identity and no means to interface with the ever-changing circumstances they encounter as they journey through life. To our detriment and the detriment of others, distorted and discordant patterns of thought and feeling have carelessly been passed from one unsuspecting and unseeing generation of human beings to the next. These destructive patterns of thought and feeling have been imprinted in memory and needlessly continue to govern and influence how we interface with others, the world and ourselves. As long as these distorted and discordant thoughts and feelings remain unacknowledged, blindly accepted, and thoughtlessly unchecked, they will unerringly continue to reproduce the tragic state in which humanity now finds itself. Arthur Schopenhauer, the German philosopher advises, "It is very necessary that a man should be appraised early in life that it is a masquerade in which he finds himself, for otherwise, there are many things which he will fail to understand." The question then arises, 'If how we now see ourselves and how we interface with others and the world is regulated and governed by the content of our memory, wouldn't the wise course of action be to question the verity of the contents of our memory?' Your liberation from the continued destructive repercussions of this "masquerade" rests solely in your continued willingness to impartially observe and candidly acknowledge, without indulging in self-condemnation and self-loathing, your personal collection of distorted and discordant thoughts and feelings as they arise in each moment. Followed by your *conscious deliberate choice* to no longer be willing to allow these previously unacknowledged and unchecked destructive patterns of thought and feeling to govern your behavior, what you think, say and do.

> "Man's life begins only with the appearance of rational consciousness."
>
> Leo Tolstoy

Imagine a scenario where you find yourself standing face-to-face with another person and they say, "You don't realize it, but, you are asleep!" and then mysteriously walk away. In an instant, those eight words are immediately interpreted by your internal dictionary, where the meanings you have given to those particular words are recorded. Based upon the meaning you have given to the word *asleep,* you wonder what that person is talking about. Remember, the whole cognitive process of you interpreting and reacting to what was just said to you takes place in a fraction of a second. You are standing there with eyes wide open…how is it possible that you could be awake and asleep at the same time? Being the curious sort, you ask yourself, "What did that person mean...*you are asleep?*" The answer to that question is found by redefining and broadening the meaning you have heretofore given to what it means for a person to be asleep. For most the meaning of the word *asleep* simply refers to a state where a person is sleeping, dormant and inactive. Curiously, as we have already noted, many of the world's greatest thinkers, prophets and sages have also chosen to use the word *asleep* to explain and reveal why human beings continue to inexplicably behave so destructively towards each other, their environment and themselves.

So, what are these great thinkers, prophets and sages attempting to convey when they say human beings are asleep? The key to you gaining a new and greater understanding of what it means to be *asleep* is found in your willingness to recognize and acknowledge that the bulk of information that is currently stored in your faculty of memory is seriously flawed. It is this seriously flawed information that you have heretofore unwittingly been identified with, providing you with a distorted and fractured sense of identity, and to your personal detriment and the detriment of others has unwittingly been allowed to govern your behavior. It is your continued and heretofore unwitting identification with this flawed information that perpetuates the tragic "masquerade" mentioned earlier. Before we proceed any further in our investigation of the faculty of memory it is vitally important for you to recognize the following fact, *YOU are **not** the flawed information that is currently stored in your faculty of memory.*

> "Never say any man is helpless, because he only represents a character, a bundle of habits, and these can be checked by new and better ones."
>
> Vivekananda

> "You can know who you are by having the great courage and honesty of seeing who you are *not*."
>
> Vernon Howard

> "Nothing except your own lack of insight compels you to remain as you are."
>
> Huang-Po

It is human beings continued unwitting identification with who they are *not* that perpetuate the fallen state of human consciousness. The present troubled state of the world is simply the out-picturing of the present troubled state of human consciousness. Human beings were not created by Life to lead tumultuous lives filled with ghastly pain and perpetual confusion. The pain and confusion can be permanently eliminated from one's life, but it will require an individual who has the courage to honestly face the disordered and fractured condition that presently exists within their *own* state of consciousness. William Law, the British theological writer, recognized that we need not look anywhere outside ourselves to find the cause for the misery and confusion we experience as individuals and as a collective. "Our salvation consists wholly in being saved from ourselves." In order to eliminate the misery and confusion in our lives, to know "salvation," we must be willing to acknowledge, even if only tentatively at first, that we are in fact the cause of our own misery and confusion. Without our acceptance of that fact we remain subject to the host of involuntary behavior patterns we have heretofore unwittingly allowed to govern and direct our lives. In Ralph Waldo Emerson's essay, Spiritual Laws, he concluded, "We are full of mechanical actions." As long as these destructive involuntary (mechanical) behavior patterns remain unacknowledged and unchecked we needlessly and repeatedly continue to experience the misery and confusion that results from their uncontrolled involuntary operation. *When these destructive behavior patterns become involuntary, performed without conscious control, have become habitual and mechanical, providing the sole basis for an individual's [my] behavior, at that point, although outwardly appearing to be awake they are in fact fast "asleep."* Throughout history when the word *asleep* was used by prophets and sages to explain the cause for the troubled state of mankind they were alluding to the description outlined in the italicized sentence you just read. Please, slowly reread the *italicized* sentence and allow its meaning to sink in. With a new understanding of what it means for a person to be *asleep* you now have a basis to begin the process whereby you can free yourself, once and for all, from your heretofore unwitting subjection to the destructive behavior patterns that have surreptitiously governed your life.

> "Who then is free? The wise man who can govern himself."
>
> Horace

> "Nothing can trouble him more, nothing can move him, for he has cut all the thousand cords of will which hold us bound to the world…as desire, fear, envy, anger, drag us here and there in constant pain. He now looks back smiling and at rest on the delusions of the world, which once were able to move and agonize his spirit also."
>
> Arthur Schopenhauer

As long as a person's life continues to be falsely governed by uncontrolled, habituated, involuntary, destructive behavior patterns, they will never be "free," they will continue to experience the tragic consequences that result from remaining asleep. The tragic state of the world bears witness to the fact that human beings have "slumbered upon themselves" (quote by Walt Whitman) for a considerable period of time, so long in fact that human beings have consequently forgotten their True Identity and by so doing have separated themselves from Life's harmonious Grand Design. At present your true identity remains sequestered behind a "veil," an illusory veil that consists of nothing more than your continued misidentification with, and unquestioned acceptance of the destructive misinformation that is currently retained in your faculty of memory.

> "The great mystery to me is how I could have been asleep to all this for so many years. I can now see what finally happened – I simply refused to go along with my old and agonizing life any longer."
>
> Vernon Howard

CHAPTER 4

Exploring the Darkness Within You

When we observe the external world we find two divisions, we have the *natural world* and the *man-made world*. The natural world is easily distinguishable from the man-made world. The natural world is produced by Life, whereas the man-made world is produced by man. Similarly, in the act of observing oneself it becomes obvious that we also live in two worlds at the same time. There is the *external world* consisting of the earth and its inhabitants and then there is our *private inner world* which is composed of our personal collection of acquired thoughts and feelings. The composition of your private inner world is commensurate with the heterogeneous mass of acquired information which is currently retained in your faculty of memory. This seamless, all-inclusive matrix of acquired information constitutes the infrastructure for an individual's private inner world. As one lives and moves about in the external world, how they define, view, interpret and interface with the external world is strictly governed by the mass of acquired information that is retained in their faculty of memory. It is from this heterogeneous mass of acquired information that our sense of identity is derived; it is also wholly responsible for providing the data/information we utilize and depend upon to guide us as we navigate our daily lives.

The meanings and definitions we assign to everything we observe in the external world are determined by the meanings and definitions we have assigned to them in our private inner world. As we look out at the external world we are in fact looking at the external world from the perspective of our private inner world. How we "see" and respond to the external world is determined by the information that is stored in our faculty of memory. The following story illustrates. Two young boys were invited to a horse ranch by the ranches' owner. Upon arrival the owner asked the boys if they would like to tour the ranch. They both replied, "Ok!" As they walked around the ranch both boys were equally attentive as the owner showed them how a horse ranch operates. The last stop on the tour was the stables. The first stall they approached was horseless and wall-to-wall with a thick layer of horse manure. The first young boy looked into the stall and then with a disgusted look on his face, exclaimed, "Gross!" and walked away. The second boy upon looking into the stall started clapping his hands and jumping up and down with glee. The owner a bit dumbfounded by the boy's gleeful reaction asked, "What is making you so happy?" With an ear to ear smile the gleeful young boy looked expectantly up into the owner's eyes and said, "With all this horse manure there has to be pony around here somewhere!" The point of this little story is simply to illustrate how the content of memory governs how we interpret and respond to external circumstances. In the above story the circumstance the boys encountered was the same, yet their behaviors were entirely different. By gaining just a basic understanding as to how your faculty of memory functions, you will now be more able to *consciously observe* the operation of your memory as it governs your behavior, what you think, say and do. Your life will become less and less bewildering as you diligently practice, study, and consciously observe the moment to moment operation of your mind, passively observing the thoughts and feelings as they rise to the surface of your conscious awareness in each moment.

"It is necessary to study the mind itself, mind studying mind. We know that there is a power of the mind called reflective. I am talking to you; at the same time I am standing aside, as it were, a second person, and knowing and hearing what I am talking. You work and think at the same time. Another portion of your mind stands by and sees what you are talking. The powers of the mind should be concentrated and turned back upon itself, and as the darkest places reveal their secrets before the penetrating rays of the sun, so will this concentrated mind penetrate its own innermost secrets."

Vivekananda

"I am in the process of bringing all my defects into the light for the purpose of getting rid of them."

Charles Henault

Charles Henault recognized that in order to rid himself of "defects" it required that they first be brought into the light; the light of conscious awareness. The meaning of the word *defects* can easily be misconstrued. For a person to view themselves as "defective" in some way or another is a form of highly toxic self-condemnation and self-loathing which imprisons that person within the toxicant view they have of themselves. However, when a person honestly and consciously, *without* self-condemnation and self-loathing, is finally willing to recognize and acknowledge the darkness that exists within themselves they concurrently start the evolving process whereby they can free themselves from the deeply seated patterns of self-deception that have kept them bound. Carl Jung the Swiss psychiatrist and father of analytical psychology determined, "One does not become enlightened by imagining figures of light, but by making the darkness conscious." In the external world when something is brought out of the darkness into the light that provides the opportunity to see what was previously unseen and unrecognized. In the process of bringing something into the light we must logically conclude that the *thing* being brought into the light was formerly in darkness, unseen. Interestingly, the word *darkness* is another term that has frequently been used by sages and prophets down through ages to illuminate the cause for the arduously repetitive human condition. What is it that constitutes the darkness these wise men are referring to? Where does the darkness reside within an individual? Is darkness necessary in order to experience the Light? Before a person can once again dwell-in and experience the Light, they first must be willing to avow within themselves the incontrovertible FACT that the darkness resides nowhere other than within themselves. Your conscious awareness and conscious acknowledgement of the darkness within you is the necessary first step for anyone desiring to be free of the darkness within them. To continue to look outside oneself for the darkness will guarantee the perpetuation of the troublesome conditions the darkness within *them* is responsible for producing. Let us dig deeper and see if we can gain a greater understanding as to the nature of darkness.

Before starting our examination into the perplexing and misunderstood nature of darkness it is crucial that you regard what we discover about darkness *only* in relationship to the darkness that at present resides within *you*. If you choose to continue to deny and refuse to face the darkness that presently resides within you, you will needlessly be condemning yourself to a life that remains governed by the involuntary and mechanical operation of the unacknowledged darkness residing within you. It is in your conscious recognition, "making the darkness conscious," (quote by Carl Jung) that you have the opportunity to no longer be subject to its deleterious effect upon your life. Moreover, it is not your job to point out and try and remove the darkness in others, each person is totally responsible for doing their own inner work. Each person frees themselves by first having the willingness and courage to face the darkness that presently resides within them, followed by their deliberate conscious choice to no longer allow the darkness they discover within to continue to surreptitiously govern their behavior, what they think, say and do. The above two steps constitute a *process;* a means to achieve a desired end. As you begin to understand the process whereby your freedom can be achieved, you must never loose sight of the fact that the onus for your "deliverance" rests solely in your hands. In order to free yourself you must be willing to wholeheartedly immerse yourself in this life saving process until the darkness within you has been completely dispelled. Your continued wholehearted immersion into this life saving process insures that you will no longer remain under the hypnotic "spell" of the unacknowledged darkness that has heretofore been governing your life. Quite literally, your "seeing" of the darkness, precedes your freeing.

> "The first thing to do is to understand the rule; the second thing is to learn the practice of it. The theory may be understood at once by an effort of reason, and yet the practice of it acquired only in the course of time."
>
> Arthur Schopenhauer

"If you want to be an astronomer you must go to the observatory, take a telescope, study the stars and planets, and then you will become an astronomer. Each science must have its own methods. I could preach you thousands of sermons but they would not make you religious, until you first practiced the method. These are the truths of the sages of all countries, of all ages, men pure and unselfish, who had no motive but to do good to the world. They all declare that they have found some higher truth than that the senses can bring to us, and they challenge verification. They say to you, take up the method and practice honestly…So we must work faithfully, using the prescribed methods, and Light will come."

Vivekananda

"Practice yourself, for heaven's sake, in little things, and then proceed to the greater."

Epictetus

Let us continue our exploration of the darkness by using an analogy between the memory in a computer and the faculty of memory in a human being. The memory in a computer and *all* the information contained within its memory can be likened to an archive that contains the complete history of the computer. If the computer was a sentient being the information archived in its memory could be regarded as the computer's "personal history." When the computer was first purchased, new out of the box, its memory only contained the information that was relative to its overall mechanical operation. For purposes of this analogy, all *subsequent information* downloaded into the computers memory should be regarded as the computer's personal history. The computer's personal history and the totality of the subsequent information downloaded into its memory banks are one and the same. Now, we have two aspects relative to the operation of the computer's memory. First, we have the information stored in its memory that is necessary for the mechanical operation of the computer provided by the original manufacture. Next, we have all the subsequent information that was downloaded into the computer's memory banks throughout the life of the computer, its personal history. Both aspects of memory are absolutely necessary, but it is the content of the subsequent information held in memory that provides the sole basis for the computer's ability to "think" and interface with the cyber world. Clearly, without the subsequent information that gets *permanently* stored in the computer's memory banks, the operation of the computer would be equivalent to a person experiencing a state of complete amnesia or the advanced stages of Alzheimer's. One of the greatest fears associated with owning a computer is the complete erasure of its memory. Again, if the computer was a sentient being the erasure of its memory would be equivalent to it loosing its sense of identity, its intellect, its personality, its personal history, its personal relatedness to others and the world. The point of this analogy is to not only underscore the pivotal role the memory plays in both computers and human beings, but to bring attention to the FACT that what we each refer to as "my" world and the contents of our faculty of memory (heart) are one and the same. EVERY facet and aspect of your *private inner world* resides within your faculty of memory!

> "Each heart is a world. You find all within yourself that you find without. The world that surrounds you is the magic glass of the world within you."
>
> Johann Lavater

Next to the fear of erasure of memory the fear of our computer contracting a virus is a major concern. When the information in a computer's memory becomes contaminated due to a virus or for some other reason the accuracy of its output becomes distorted, its "behavior" becomes erratic and deleterious. If the distorted information in the computer's memory remains undetected and unacknowledged the repercussions caused by its lack of detection and acknowledgement could result in catastrophic consequences.

Billions upon billions of dollars are spent annually worldwide to insure the protection of the information contained in the memory banks of computers around the world. Anyone whose livelihood relies on the flawless operation of their computer recognizes the vital importance of keeping the contents of its memory free from contamination and loss.

The operation of the human mental apparatus, the human "bio-computer," is basically no different than a computer purchased from HP, Dell, or IBM. Where do you think human beings got the idea for a computer in the first place? It is the content of memory in each one, whether human or store bought, that determines what their output will be. The familiar saying, "garbage in garbage out," applies equally to both the human bio-computer and the commercial variety. Tragically, countless generations of human beings have failed to recognize that the information that is currently contained within their faculty of memory, both individually and collectively is severely contaminated. Year after year, century after century, millennium after millennium, this severely contaminated information continues to be thoughtlessly "downloaded," and repetitiously passed from one unsuspecting generation to the next. Thus, it continues to provide the basis for all the erratic and deleterious patterns of thought and feeling that characterize human behavior, commonly referred to as human nature. No one is exempt, all of mankind at present is immersed and imprisoned within this well established toxic stew. The "pot" that harbors this toxic stew is the faculty of memory. *The continued undetected and unchecked operation of this pernicious toxic stew within an individual is synonymous with that individual living in a state of perpetual "darkness."* Human beings were not created by Life to be mindless, bewildered creatures who fumble around in darkness day after day, destroying themselves, each other, and the planet. As long as the darkness remains unacknowledged and unchecked it will unerringly continue to reproduce the troubled state human beings have been experiencing for untold ages.

What revealing insights and discoveries have we made into the perplexing nature of darkness? So far, we have ascertained that the darkness's place of residence is within the faculty of memory. Additionally, we have discovered that the darkness is a "toxic stew" which is composed of the severely contaminated information that is currently stored in memory, that has the ability to directly influence and govern our lives when left unacknowledged and unchecked. One crucial question that remains to be answered in our investigation of darkness is this. What is it that constitutes the darkness and how can *it* be dispelled? Anyone who presupposes that they understand what darkness *is* by merely saying to themselves: "The darkness is the severely contaminated information in my faculty of memory," is sidestepping the absolute necessity for identifying and acknowledging the darkness that exists within them at the present time. In order for the darkness to be dispelled it first must be observed within ourselves. As you become consciously aware and awaken to the fact of the darkness's existence within you and the deleterious effect it is having upon your life and the life of others, you are now faced with a life altering choice. You can lethargically acquiesce and fall back "asleep" and continue to allow the familiar and well rehearsed darkness to surreptitiously govern your life, or you can make the conscious choice and refuse to allow your life to any longer be governed by the darkness. Step by step, a new world gradually emerges for those who choose to stay awake and courageously face the darkness within them.

> "Take no part in the unfruitful works of darkness, but instead expose them."
>
> Ephesians 5:11

"The first lesson, then, is to sit for some time and let the mind run on. The mind is bubbling up all the time. It is like a monkey jumping about. Let the monkey jump as much as he can; you simply watch and wait. Knowledge is power says the proverb, and that is true. Until you know what the mind is doing you cannot control it. Give it the full length of the reins; many of the most hideous thoughts [darkness] may come into it; you will be astonished that it was possible for you to think such thoughts. But you will find that each day the mind's vagaries are becoming less and less violent, that each day it is becoming calmer…until at last it will be under perfect control, but we must patiently practice every day."

Vivekananda

Getting to the *Heart* of the Matter

CHAPTER 5

Dispelling the Darkness within You

"And ye shall know the truth, and the truth shall make you free."

John 8:32

The title of this chapter is, *Dispelling the Darkness within You*. It is not, *Dispelling the Darkness within your Neighbor*. Attempting to dispel the darkness in someone other than yourself is an unnecessary distraction which will only delay your inner progress. When the darkness has been dispelled from within you, then and only then, will you be in a position to offer assistance to others. A wise teacher of men instructed, "Thou hypocrite, first cast out the beam out of thine own eye; and then shalt thou see clearly to cast out the mote out of thy brother's eye!" Let us continue, keeping the above instruction foremost in our mind as we seek to answer the following question that was raised in the last chapter.

'What is it that constitutes the darkness and how can it be dispelled?'

In our investigation of darkness, it is vitally important to keep in mind the distinction that exists between our invisible *private inner world* and the visible *external world* of form. Remember, as we look out upon the external world, we are looking at the external world from the perspective provided by our private inner world. How we respond to the circumstances we encounter in the external world are conditioned by the massive cluster of acquired thoughts and feelings that are currently stored in memory. This voluminous array of acquired thoughts and feelings provide the basis for a person's sense of identity and likewise furnishes the "support data" used by that person to direct their journey through life. The composition of your private inner world and this vast array of acquired thoughts and feelings stored in memory are equivalent. What is the actual nature and quality of your private thoughts and feelings? It is by gaining a deeper understanding into the actual nature and quality of your private thoughts and their associative feelings that you start the process of dispelling the darkness within. As you courageously face the falsehood and distortions that exists within your own thoughts and feelings, the darkness is gradually dispelled, your perception is subsequently clarified, and you "see" both your private inner world and external world through new eyes.

When observing ourselves and others what are the basic components that go into the makeup of an individual's invisible private inner world? The makeup of a person's private inner world is composed of three basic components. We have two components that are commonly referred to as our *thoughts* and *feelings*, and the generally overlooked and often ignored third component which is the enigmatic, ever present, animating Life Force. Obviously, it is this ever-present, animating Life Force that is the very source of our lives, without which thought and feeling would be impossible.

When a baby is born into the world it is not difficult to be deeply moved by their innocence and complete lack of falsehood; they are "transparent." Generally, there is nothing blocking or distorting the Life Force as it freely radiates out into the world through their tiny body. Their innocence is palpable. Their faculty of memory much like the memory in a store-bought computer only contains the "built-in" programming supplied by Life that is relevant to the continued overall functioning and growth of their body. As we're all well aware it is not long before the child's unsullied faculty of memory starts to be impregnated and filled with all sorts of distorted and discordant patterns of thought and feeling that characterize the human nature state. Clearly, a young child has not yet developed the capacity whereby they can filter-out or reject the distorted and discordant and adulterated information that is carelessly being downloaded into their memory. As the child continues to grow and develop physically, concurrently, the data being downloaded into the child's faculty of memory continues to expand and develop; a unique personality develops, which is given a name. As the child matures this mass of acquired information will provide the sole basis for their personal sense of identity and also the support data they will submit to and rely on for guidance as they interface with the world.

How each person interfaces with the external world and how they privately "see" themselves internally is governed by the nature and quality of the acquired information stored in their faculty of memory. When how we interface with the external world and how we privately see ourselves is permitted to be unconsciously governed and determined by the distorted and discordant patterns of thought and feeling we have acquired throughout our life, we unwittingly and needlessly continue to submit to living our life in "darkness." It is only through our very personal and private acknowledgement of our present *internal condition* that we can ever hope to free ourselves from the darkness. As long as you remain under the hypnotic "spell" cast by the darkness within you, you will needlessly be relegating yourself to a life that will remain subject to the pernicious dictates of that very darkness. William Law beseeched his readership to employ the following instruction. "Only let your present and past distress make you feel and acknowledge this twofold great truth: First, that in and of yourself, you are nothing but darkness, vanity, and misery; Secondly, that of yourself, you can no more help yourself to light and comfort, than you can create an angel. People at all times can seem to assent [agree] to these two truths, but then it is an assent that has no depth or reality [conviction], and so is of little or no use, but your condition has opened your heart for a deep and full conviction of these truths. Now give way, I beseech you, to this conviction, and hold these two truths, in the same degree of certainty as you know two and two to be four, and then you are with the prodigal (prodigal son mentioned in the Bible) come to yourself, and above half your work is done." You "come to yourself," the experience of your True Identity, by having the courage to face the darkness that at present resides within you, which you have mistakenly been identified with and heedlessly allowed to surreptitiously govern your life. The darkness must first be seen and acknowledged before it can be dispelled. When the darkness is clearly seen and acknowledged, then, more than "half your work" in the process of freeing yourself is done. Step by step, as the layers of heretofore unseen darkness are exposed to the light of your conscious awareness, you increasingly delight and give thanks that Life affords you the opportunity, IF YOU CHOOSE, to no longer be identified-with and governed-by the unseen darkness within.

> "There is no greater delight than to be conscious of sincerity in self- examination."
>
> Mencius

"Use the light that is in you to recover your natural clearness of sight."

> Lao-tse

"No one can conquer an enemy without coming in sight of him."

> Emanuel Swedenborg

"If you did not desire your present position, you would not be doing everything possible to maintain it…If you cease doing those things which maintain your position, you will lose at once that position which you claim is forced upon you and which is your burden."

> Leo Tolstoy

When we look out upon the *natural world* we observe a seamless, living, operational system that extends far beyond what we can see with our eyes; one unfathomable whole comprised of a myriad of interrelated parts, which is commonly referred to as Creation. When we observe this Operational Living System we call Creation what are the fundamental attributes that makeup its composition? At the fundamental level there are three primary attributes which we can easily recognize. One, there is an invisible ever-present Source of Energy that ceaselessly animates and maintains the entire living system. The entire living system is continually bathed and enfolded in this Energy. Second, the entire Living System is a meticulously coordinated functional Design which gives indication that a Greater Intelligence than the human intellect possess was involved in designing It and bringing It forth. Third, there are timeless immutable Laws and Principles that govern and control the entire living system, insuring the continued harmonious operation of the entire system. What is referred to as Creation is the ongoing perpetual harmonious operation of this Living System.

By way of comparison let us take note of the differences between the natural world and the man-made world. When we look out upon the man-made world what do we observe?

When looked at honestly and without judgment the man-made world is a severely fragmented, dysfunctional, dying system that encompasses the entire planet. This man-made world is commonly referred to by human beings as a highly advanced technological civilization. To further our comparison between the natural world and the man-made world let us look at the three primary attributes that constitute the makeup of the man-made world. One, the entire man-made world is kept "energized" through man's systematic and deliberate plundering of the natural world's finite resources. This humanly contrived man-made system for energy production is constantly being threatened by a multitude of factors which have the potential to drastically effect energy production. If energy production ceases, the man-made world will simultaneously crumble and cease to exist. Second, the overall design of the man-made world is a disjointed collection of uncoordinated and disharmonious parts which is subject to total collapse at any moment. The fragile ramshackle design of the man-made world gives indication that human beings are not as intelligent as they might imagine. The design of the man-made world is simply an external out-manifestation which precisely reflects and clearly reveals the severely fragmented and dysfunctional state that at present exists within human consciousness. Third, the laws and moral principles that have been formulated by human beings to govern and control the man-made world are transitory and mutable. The man-made laws and moral principles that are presently in force are based upon the prevailing attitudes as to what is considered to be right or wrong behavior. Since there is no agreed upon standard for what constitutes right and wrong behavior throughout the man-made world the entire man-made world remains in a state of perpetual conflict and division.

The above two paragraphs provide a cursory glimpse into the comparative differences between the natural world and the man-made world. Both the natural world and the man-made world are complete systems unto themselves. The natural world is a complete operational system produced by Life, while the man-made world is a complete operational system produced by human beings on the surface of the planet. The grievous man-made world system established on the surface of the planet is the direct *effect* of the operation of the darkened state of the human intellect. Vivekananda, the Indian Hindu monk openly declared, "The external world is but the gross form of the internal, or subtle. The finer is always the cause, and the grosser the effect. So, the external world is the effect, and the internal the cause. In the same way external forces are simply the grosser parts, of which the internal forces are the finer. One who has discovered and learned how to manipulate the internal forces will get the whole of nature under his control…He will be master of the whole of nature, internal and external." Tragically, human beings continue to suffer under the deeply ingrained illusory belief that the machinations of the human intellect, which are responsible for producing the grievous man-made world, will also be able to provide "answers" to the problems those very same intellectual machinations were responsible for producing.

What is Vivekananda referring to when he speaks of an internal force that is the "cause" for what is brought forth in the external world? What invisible internal force is in operation in both the natural world and the man-made world, without which, the manifestations we observe in the external world could not have been created? It is the operation of "intellectual force," thought-in-action, relative to the objects being created externally that *is* the internal force, which precedes and gives rise to all the multitudinous forms of manifestation in the external world. The operation of the intellect within a human being can be regarded as a dynamic and powerful mental force, the internal cause, that is responsible for all the external effects we see manifested around us in the external man-made world.

> "All that a man does outwardly is but the expression and completion of his inward thought. To work effectually, he must think clearly; to act nobly, he must think nobly. Intellectual force is the principle element of the soul's life and should be proposed by every man as the principle end of his being."
>
> William E. Channing

When we look out upon the external world what do observe? We see a state of separation that exists between the natural world and the man-made world. Clearly, the man-made world is not in harmony with the natural world. Why? The reason for the lack of harmony between natural world and the man-made world becomes obvious when looked at in terms of the *nature of the intelligence* that gives rise to what has been brought forth in each of these worlds. The nature of the intelligence that gives rise to the creation of the man-made world can be found by inquiring into the nature of the human intellect. Correspondingly, the nature of the intelligence that gives rise to the creation of the natural world can be found by inquiring into the nature of a Greater Intelligence which is responsible for maintaining and bringing into manifestation the entire Living Creation. Both the external man-made world and the external natural world are simply reflections that reveal the nature of the intelligence that was responsible for bringing them forth into manifestation. Human beings continued experience of separation from the natural world, from Life, is due solely to their failure to recognize the following fact. The fact is, by unconsciously kowtowing to the ruinous urgings of the seriously adulterated human intellect, human beings needlessly condemn themselves to re-experiencing the confusion, misery and suffering produced by their continued lack of wakefulness. Human beings protracted lack of being wakeful is synonymous with human beings living in a state of perpetual darkness. The severely adulterated contents of the collective human intellect, the collective darkness, has heedlessly been passed down from one unsuspecting generation of human beings to the next for untold ages; unerringly reproducing the tragic man-made world that results when human beings continue to exist in a somnolent state where the operation of the darkness in human lives remains unobserved and unchecked.

The dispelling of the darkness within you is at hand! If you have allowed yourself to openly receive and assimilate the ideas contained in the preceding chapters, you now have in your personal possession the fundamental information which will assist you in the process of dispelling the darkness within you. With your new found understanding as to the nature of darkness and how it operates within you, you now have the unprecedented opportunity to no longer allow the darkness to dictate how you view and interpret life or to direct and govern your moment to moment behavior. The mystery that once tightly enshrouded the nature and origin of darkness has been removed. Your new understanding into the nature and origin of darkness *is* your protection from the darkness's heretofore unrecognized and unacknowledged deleterious effect upon your life. From this point forward in your life, your personal identification and relationship with the darkness within you will no longer be the same! No longer will the operation of the darkness within you go undetected and unseen; UNLESS YOU CHOOSE to "close your eyes" and lethargically fall back into a state of nightmarish slumber. The choice is yours! No longer can you proclaim, "I just didn't know!"

> "You have not known what you are; you have slumbered upon yourself all your life…Whoever you are! Claim your own."
>
> Walt Whitman

> "He who learns the rules of wisdom, without conforming to them in his life, is like a man who labors in his field, but did not sow."
>
> Saadi

Getting to the *Heart* of the Matter

CHAPTER 6

The Process of Reawakening to Reality

"To be awake is to be alive…We must learn to reawaken and keep ourselves awake, not by mechanical aids, but by an infinite expectation of the dawn."

Henry David Thoreau

The process of awakening to Reality is just that a *process;* more specifically a creative process. With regard to all Life oriented creative processes, from the formation of the planets in the cosmos, to the formation of a blade of grass here on Earth, there are immutable laws and principles that govern each step of the ongoing creative process. In the process of reawakening to Reality the same exact laws and principles that govern the operation of the cosmos, likewise, govern the process of our reawakening to Reality. Our reawakening to Reality is a creative process. The fulfillment of that reawakening process can only be realized when orchestrated and governed by the operation of a Greater Intelligence; the Greater Intelligence that IS, which is responsible for the creation of the entire Cosmos. The repeated futile attempts by the shortsighted human intellect to *awaken itself* are tantamount to a person trying to pick themselves up by their own bootstraps. In the case of the person trying to pick themselves up by their own bootstraps it is evident that a greater power than themselves is required if they wish to rise up off the ground. Correspondingly, in the process of your reawaking to Reality, in order to for you rise up out of your present darkened state will require the guidance and power provided by a Greater Intelligence; the Intelligence of Life. In his book, *The Meditations,* Marcus Aurelius makes reference in the following quote to the importance of revering the power and intelligence that is responsible for creating and maintaining the natural world. "Every instrument, tool and vessel, if it does that for which it has been made, is well, and yet he who made it is not there. But in things that are put together by *nature* there abides in them the power which made them, therefore, the more correct it is to reverence this power. Think that if you live and act according to *its* will, everything in you is in harmony with *its* intelligence. And thus, also in the universe the things which belong to *it* are in conformity to *its* intelligence."

Human beings were "put together by nature," by Life, to be part of, and take part in, the ongoing creative processes relative to planet Earth. Can you think of any other reason or purpose for our existence as human beings? It is extremely illogical and arrogant to assume that the Greater Intelligence that created human beings would have created such a beautiful planet with the intention of having those very same human beings desecrate and destroy it. Yet, human beings have taken it upon themselves to do exactly that. It is what human beings have chosen to do, both individually and collectively, that has created the tragic state of affairs currently being experienced worldwide by mankind. What is it that governs and controls what human beings do? More importantly, what is it that determines what *you* do? What controls and governs what *you* think, say and do; what you express? Moment by moment what determines how you interpret and evaluate the circumstances you encounter as you journey through life?

The key word in all of the above questions is the word *you*. Deeply consider the following profound idea in relationship to yourself. When born into the world, "*you*" as you now know yourself did not exist! The formation of your private inner world, with *you* at its center, had not yet evolved and taken form in consciousness. The personal sense of identity that you presently accept and regard as *you* was nonexistent. The personal story that you now refer to as "my" life story had not yet been written and imprinted upon your heart. If the story of your life was published today as a book the title would be, '*The Private Inner World of* _____.' Fill in the blank space with your first name. Now take a few moments and stand back and look at your personal life story, your private inner world of thoughts and feelings, from the perspective of an impartial observer. What do you see? It is vitally important that as you observe yourself you do not form opinions about what you find. In addition, don't allow yourself to fall into the subtle mental trap of judging yourself regardless of what you may observe when practicing this simple exercise. Simply observe and become aware of what's there without forming any kind of mental judgment or conclusion whatsoever. For example, if you start judging yourself as being, good or evil, wonderful or despicable, capable or incapable, ugly or beautiful, lovable or unlovable, spiritually superior or spiritually inferior, stupid or brilliant, etc., etc., etc., you will immediately become psychologically subject to your own judgments. Additionally, don't forget to include all your judgments as they relate to other people and the world at large.

Make your own Judgment Journal. Your Judgment Journal will consist of three separate lists. The first list will be titled – "HOW I JUDGE MYSELF;" the second list will be titled – "HOW I JUDGE OTHERS;" and the third list will be titled – "HOW I JUDGE THE WORLD AT LARGE." Practice this journaling exercise in private. If you commit yourself to this journaling process you will quickly discover you need more than one sheet of paper for each list. As you practice this exercise you will discover that psychologically you have been held captive by nothing more than your own misguided judgments of yourself, others and the world at large. The biblical injunction given in Matthew 7:2, cautions, that as we judge we become subject to our own judgments. "For with what judgment ye judge, ye shall be judged: and with what measure ye mete [assign], it shall be measured to you again."

Our personal judgments form the psychological basis for how we have learned to "see" ourselves, others and the world at large, then, we proceed to live our lives based upon what we "see."

> "If you are pained by any external thing, it is not this thing that disturbs you, but your own judgment about it. It is in your power to erase this judgment now. If anything in your own nature gives you pain, who hinders you from correcting your opinion?"
>
> Marcus Aurelius

As long as your sense of identity remains intimately intertwined with your personal story you will remain subject to the script that has been written upon your heart. The first step in setting yourself free is to start the gradual and deliberate process wherein you no longer believe-in or identify-with the story you tell yourself about yourself, others and the world at large. As long as you continue to maintain your personal collection of misguided judgments and false beliefs about yourself, others and the world, you will continue to remain subject to the limitations and distortions inherent within those very beliefs. You set yourself free by letting go of your identification with your personal story. As you deliberately cease being identified with your personal story, you gradually become consciously aware that your True Identity, the True You is what was born into the world BEFORE your personal story was ever written upon your heart and judged by you to be true.

Has anyone ever seen intelligence? We are able to see the visible results of the operation of intelligence, thought-in-action; in both the man-made world and the natural world, but as to the actual composition of that intelligence it remains invisible to the naked eye in both cases. It is not difficult when observing the man-made world and the natural world to discern that the humanly fashioned intelligence that brought forth the man-made world is not in harmony with the Greater Intelligence that brought forth the natural world. Furthermore, we must humbly acknowledge that the Greater Intelligence that brought forth the natural world pre-existed the diminutive pool of humanly configured intelligence that is responsible for bringing forth the man-made world. When looking at both the natural world and the man-made world from the above perspective what do we observe? It becomes evident that countless generations of slumbering human beings have misused their capacity of intellect, mulishly attempting to create a substitute man-made world to take the place of the natural world. To quote Vernon Howard an American born esoteric philosopher, "It is man's frantic insistence upon substitutes which releases the flood of folly upon the earth." In man's repeated, self-willed attempts to create the "perfect world" for themselves, human beings have only succeeded in widening the gap between themselves and natural world. As this gap continues to widen the future survival of mankind becomes more and more uncertain. The precarious state in which human beings now find themselves *will not* and *cannot* be remedied by the capricious machinations of the diminutive human intellect regardless of how high sounding they might appear. Albert Einstein's insightful quotes which penetrate deeply into the nature and cause for the present human condition bears repeating, "We cannot solve our problems with the same thinking we used when we created them." and "Insanity is doing the same thing over and over again and expecting different results."

In the process of your reawakening to Reality it is vitally important that you begin to recognize the differences that exist between the nature of the intelligence that brought forth the man-made world and the nature of the Greater Intelligence that brought forth the natural world. In the last chapter the most obvious differences that exist between these two states was addressed. Before reading any further, take a few moments and go back to the last chapter and reread the paragraphs where the comparative differences between the man-man world and the natural world were explored. When finished, return to this page and continue reading.

The words *reawakening to Reality* give indication that human being *can* awaken from the well entrenched darkened state in which they now exist into a state which is commonly referred to as Reality. So, what is the meaning of the word *Reality*? The word *Reality* is the word used to describe the Totality of all things contained within the overall design of Life. Consider the words *Life* and *Reality* as interchangeable as you continue reading. As part of its Totality the overall design of Reality is comprised of both visible and invisible aspects. The visible aspects of Reality are typically referred to by human beings as Creation or the natural world, while the invisible aspects of Reality are generally regarded by human being as "something" mysterious and unknowable. There is a vague sensing by human beings that "something" invisible must exist, but for most if they're honest there is a complete lack of personal relatedness. So instead of experiencing a sense of personal relatedness with the invisible aspects of Reality human beings experience a profound sense of separation. This profound sense of separation from Reality is experienced by human beings in consciousness.

> "You ask,' How can we know the Infinite?' I answer, not by reason. It is the office of reason to distinguish and define. The Infinite, therefore, cannot be ranked among its objects. You can apprehend the Infinite by a faculty superior to reason, by entering into a state in which you are your finite self no longer, in which the Divine Essence is communicated to you. This is Ecstasy. It is the liberation of your mind from finite consciousness."
>
> Plotinus

In many respects, the process of reawakening to Reality is comparable to a person going to sleep at night and reawakening in the morning. The person who went to sleep at night is the same person that reawakens in the morning. One moment they were asleep oblivious to what is transpiring in the world around them, the next moment they are awake and aware of what's going on in their immediate environment. It is illogical to assume that it would be possible for a slumbering individual to somehow transform their sleeping state of consciousness into the experience of an awakened state of consciousness while still asleep. The sleeping state and the awakened state are obviously mutually exclusive states of consciousness. Similarly, it is just as illogical to assume the following scenario is possible. That an individual who remains identified with their darkened state of consciousness would be capable of transforming their darkened state of consciousness into to a state of consciousness that embodies and reveals the true nature of Reality, while still remaining identified with the darkness within them.

The "substance" of consciousness is analogous to a screen in a movie theatre. Both the substance of consciousness and the screen remain in a passively receptive state until something is projected upon them. The substance of consciousness, like the movie screen, is simply a reflective medium, in effect a mirror, which will accurately reflect back to an individual whatever they happen to project upon it. What you now experience as your life is quite literally a "living, multi-sensory, holographic reflection" of what frame by frame is being projected upon the substance of consciousness. The following story will help to illustrate. Imagine a person entering a darkened movie theatre where the feature film had already begun. They take their seat and start watching the movie. After a few minutes they become very annoyed with storyline of the movie. Impulsively, they get up from their seat, run up to movie screen and start yelling at the actors and pounding their fists upon the screen. They continue to rail against the screen, but to their utter dismay nothing changes. They exit the movie theatre angry, frustrated, and confused. The movie-goer in the above story was attempting the impossible by trying to change what was being projected onto the screen. Clearly, in order to change what was being projected onto the screen the old film in the theatre's projector needs to be removed in order to make space for a new film to be installed. Additionally, cutting and re-splicing the old film would change nothing other than to rearrange the old film into an updated configuration. In the process of you reawakening to Reality the "old film" which is now providing the basis for what is being projected onto the substance of consciousness, likewise needs to be let go of and "removed" in order to make space for the New. The story of your life, which includes your present sense of identity, is comprised of the reams and reams of old film that are presently stored in your faculty of memory. Your present deeply conditioned view of life and yourself is nothing but the *PAST*, the old films, being projected onto the substance of consciousness in this now moment. For just as long as you choose to continue to identify yourself with what is being projected upon the substance of consciousness that will continue to be the experience you have of your life. The old films that are now being projected upon the substance of consciousness are made up of nothing more than the crystallized, misleading judgments and beliefs you have had about yourself, others and the world at large that are stored in memory. It is through your deliberate letting go of all misleading judgments and false beliefs that you initiate the epic process of dispelling the darkness within you. As the darkness within you is dispelled, you *gradually* reawaken from your deep slumber into the Reality that has always been present. As you cease identifying with the past, i.e. the old films, a wonderworking Life Directed Re-Creative Process is set in motion which will culminate in you experiencing a totally new state of consciousness that embodies and reveals the true nature of Reality.

> "On this road, therefore, to abandon one's own way is to enter on the true way, or, to speak more correctly, to advance to the goal…for the spirit which has courageously resolved on passing, inwardly and outwardly, beyond the limits of its own nature, enters the limitless higher world."
>
> John Yepes

"The problem is never how to get new innovative thoughts into your mind but how to get the old ones out. Every mind is a building filled with archaic furniture. Clean out a corner of your mind and creativity will instantly fill it."

Dee Hock

"What is the use of going right over the old track again? You must make tracks into the Unknown."

Henry David Thoreau

We must each make this journey into the Unknown alone. Others pilgrims who have already made the epic inner journey into the Unknown will be able to provide guidance, inspiration and encouragement, but ultimately the final decision as to whether you make tracks into the Unknown is yours. It is a very personal journey one that is driven by a deep longing in an individual to understand and experience a greater Reality than the claustrophobic one the man-made world has to offer. When that deep longing in a person is greater than the hypnotic appeal of the man-man world, then and only then, will the journey begin in earnest for that person. The journey into the Unknown is a deliberate "death march" that paradoxically delivers you into a greater experience of Life. It is the deliberate casting-off of your old nature, the "old you," you have been identified with your entire life until now. It is the deliberate letting go of the timeworn mental and emotional "grave clothes" that have kept you bound.

> "A sublime soul can rise to all kinds of greatness, but [only] by his own effort; it can tear itself loose from all bondage, to all that limits and restrains it, but only by the strength of determination."
>
> Friedrich Schiller

What does it mean to make tracks into the Unknown? Simply because something at present remains unknown to us does not mean it doesn't already exist. When a person becomes *consciously aware* of something that was previously considered unknown and it becomes known to them, in that moment of recognition they personally experience *its* existence in relationship to themselves. It may remain unknown to others, but it is known and experienced by one personally. True Knowing is a state of consciousness where there is a complete absence of "belief-about." No longer does a person experience the confusing state referred to as double-mindedness. When a person knows the Truth about something, there is no longer a need for a belief-about it. Making tracks into the Unknown is an epic inner journey that a person takes from the limited man-made "belief-about" world into the expansive and glorious ever-present world of Reality. Step-by-step, like the prodigal son, you are journeying toward your personal knowing and experience of your True Identity as a unique part in Life's Grand Design. Dare to step out of the darkness into the Light. As always, the choice is yours.

> "Cease cherishing beliefs. If you could follow this one simple instruction to its absolute conclusion, you would be enlightened, free, truth-realized.
>
> Adyashanti

Getting to the *Heart* of the Matter

EPILOGUE

"You have not known what you are; you have slumbered upon yourself all your life…Whoever you are. Claim your own."

Walt Whitman

Countless generations of human beings have lived in a darkened state of consciousness for a very long time. This darkened state of consciousness continues to be passed from one unsuspecting generation to the next; thus, it continues. What has seemed like a state of wakefulness has in fact been a protracted macabre nightmare, or a worldwide deadly affliction that is referred to in this book as a state of continuous "sleep walking." The insightful words of Leo Tolstoy bares repeating, "As a man in his sleep doubts the reality of his nightmare and yearns to awaken and return to real-life, so the average man of our day cannot, in the depth of his heart, believe the terrible condition in which he finds himself – and which is growing worse and worse - to be the reality. He yearns to attain a higher reality, the consciousness of which is already within him… Our average man has but to make a conscious effort and ask himself, 'Is not all this an illusion?' in order to feel like an awakened sleeper, transported from the hypothetical and horrible nightmare-world into a living, peaceful, and joyous world of reality."

Do you think it is negative or inappropriate to acknowledge the true state of affairs? For as long as human beings refuse to acknowledge the true state of affairs there is no starting point for a new beginning; they will continue to repeat and tenaciously hold-on-to the same old patterns of abhorrent behavior and imprudent beliefs that have thus far been able to successfully eliminate each previous generation. If we continue to delude ourselves that, somehow, we will be able to think our way out of the current mess we are in, or that we will be saved by divine intervention, both of these misguided assumptions carry the heaviest of penalties. How many civilizations have come and gone, all clinging to these same imprudent, death-dealing assumptions? Clearly, we're next, if we continue down the path we are now on.

Time is running out for mankind. What is it going to take for human beings to realize the severity of the situation now unfolding on earth? We are not playing a meaningless video game, there are life or death consequences directly related our individual and collective behavior. Who is willing to acknowledge that the present grievous state of the world is the direct result of countless generations of human beings living in a state of incessant inner darkness? Before the well-entrenched inner darkness can be dispelled it must first be acknowledged.

The meaning of the words *darkened states* and *ego-self* are equivalent. The ego-self constitutes the personification of the darkened states that reside within each individual. It is by courageously acknowledging the darkness that now resides within oneself that initiates the life-saving process referred to as *salvation*. Salvation is *not* the salvation of the human ego-self, paradoxically, it is the complete dissolution of the ego-self. It is the continued identification with the spurious ego-self that is the source of every problem that now confronts mankind. Don't expect salvation to be handed to you on a silver platter, you are totally responsible for purging the darkness that now exists within your inner kingdom – your state of consciousness. Mindful, heartfelt purging will gradually free you from all the pernicious darkened states that have been the source of all your familiar confusion and suffering. You can get off the ghastly human nature merry-go-round, but not until you are willing to honestly face the darkened states that now inhabit your inner world. Honest self-facing is most effective when immediately followed by your heartfelt resolve to no longer allow your future behavior to be governed and controlled by noxious, life-eroding darkened states of consciousness.

Now that you understand the underlying true cause for all the confusion, pain and suffering in your life and the life of others, what are you going to do with your new found understanding? LET IT BE CLEARLY UNDERSTOOD: THE PURPOSE FOR THE EPIC INNER JOURNEY IS NOT TO SAVE OR IMPROVE THE EGO-SELF, THAT WOULD ACHIEVE ABSOLUTELY NOTHING - EXCEPT TO POSSIBLY POSTPONE THE EGO-SELF'S INEVITABLE DEMISE A LITTLE WHILE LONGER. When the epic inner journey is undertaken for self-centered, selfish purposes, the imprudent pilgrim will find themselves right back where they started.

Inherent within all self-centered, self-serving behaviors are contained the seed of their eventual destruction; the world reveals this undeniable fact for anyone with eyes to see. It is quite easy to recognize and judge the dark states that exist in our fellows; to acknowledge those same dark states within oneself requires a depth of personal honesty very few human beings are willing to direct their attention to. Until there is a willingness to face the dark states that exist within ourselves, and a firm resolve to no longer allow our behavior to be governed and controlled by these ruinous dark states, the tragic world situation will remain unchanged. We each play our part in the worldwide restoration of human consciousness by deliberately letting go of the dark states that we find sequestered within ourselves. One question remains to be asked, "Are you willing to do your part?" Ultimately, the fate of mankind will be determined by how each individual chooses to respond to that question. As always, the choice is yours.

> "You need only be willing to take that first step over and over again into the unknown; your epic inner journey has now begun."
>
> RASEEDRA

STAY THE COURSE…VICTORY IS CERTAIN

Getting to the *Heart* of the Matter

About the Author

The author was born and raised in a suburb of Philadelphia, Pennsylvania. He graduated from Denver University with degrees in Business and Psychology. Upon graduation from college he enlisted in the U.S. Navy. After completing his military service, he moved to Denver, Colorado, and pursued a career in business, successfully establishing several businesses, which he continued to oversee for the next two and a half decades. He semiretired in 1994 and moved to southern Oregon, where he purchased an abandoned wilderness ranch where he lived until 2002. At present, he resides in Fort Collins, Colorado, with his partner of 33 years.

Starting in his early twenties, he developed an all-consuming desire to understand how Life was designed to work. For the past 50 years, he continued to study, explore, and search for answers to those shrouded mysteries. After a prolonged and very intense period of inner confusion and darkness, which lasted for almost seven years, the veiled answers he had so ardently searched for gradually began to appear in consciousness in the summer of 2009. In the winter of 2009 he began writing, *The Epic Inner Journey: The Choice is Yours - An*

Exploration into How Life Works. Subsequent volumes followed: *Getting to the Heart of Matter* and *The Final Choice.*

The author is simply a common man who has had an unquenchable desire to truly understand how Life *actually* works. Now, one of his greatest wishes is to share that hard-won understanding about how Life works with others, in the hope that it will be a resource that will provide assistance to the legions of courageous pilgrims who have wholeheartedly committed themselves to the process of awakening to their True Spiritual Identity.

Author's contact information: raseedra@outlook.com

The Epic Inner Journey Trilogy

These books in the Epic Journey Trilogy by Raseedra build on each other, offering the reader a developmental process that goes deeper with each book. It is therefore important for the reader to read these books in order so that they may follow the development of these ideas.

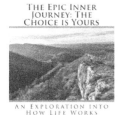

The Epic Inner Journey: The Choice is Yours

Volume I

An Exploration into How Life Works

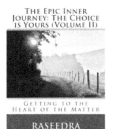

The Epic Inner Journey: The Choice is Yours

Volume II

Getting to the Heart of the Matter

The Epic Inner Journey: The Choice is Yours

Volume III

The Final Choice

Getting to the *Heart* of the Matter

Getting to the *Heart* of the Matter

Getting to the *Heart* of the Matter

Made in the USA
Las Vegas, NV
03 May 2023

71466679R00066